Asemsebe

Asemsebe

Whispers from the Ancestors

Kevin Koranteng Cheeseman

RESOURCE *Publications* · Eugene, Oregon

ASEMSEBE
Whispers from the Ancestors

Copyright © 2019 Kevin Koranteng Cheeseman. All rights reserved. Except for brief quotations in critical publications or reviews, no part of this book may be reproduced in any manner without prior written permission from the publisher. Write: Permissions, Wipf and Stock Publishers, 199 W. 8th Ave., Suite 3, Eugene, OR 97401.

Resource Publications
An Imprint of Wipf and Stock Publishers
199 W. 8th Ave., Suite 3
Eugene, OR 97401

www.wipfandstock.com

PAPERBACK ISBN: 978-1-7252-5457-2
HARDCOVER ISBN: 978-1-7252-5458-9
EBOOK ISBN: 978-1-7252-5459-6

Manufactured in the U.S.A.   NOVEMBER 20, 2019

To Vida, the two George's, and the divine Chatelle.

Time waits not for wisdom.
Therein lies the cause of all suffering.

Contents

Acknowledgements | ix

Introduction | xi

Being That | 1

Forget Me Not | 3

The Silent I | 5

Wisdom's Gain | 7

Rock Bottom | 9

Law | 11

Tide of Power | 13

Fortune | 15

In Love's Honor | 17

Easing Waters | 19

The Wheel of Causes | 21

Will Power | 22

The Call of Dawn | 24

A Shimmering Veil | 26

Decisions | 28

The Labors of Love | 31

A Pearl in The Far Lands | 33

The Sleep of Sisyphus | 35

Mortal Coil | 37

The First and Last Sound | 39

A Thousand Little Bells | 42

The Holy Instant | 43

Young Tree | 44

Innocence | 46

Age of The Reluctant Heart | 48

Acknowledgements

I have to start by thanking my wonderful wife, Chatelle. Thank you for your persistent encouragement to publish these works and for kick-starting our writing adventures. My sincere gratitude to you too B. Lynn Goodwin, author of *Never Too Late: From Wannabe to Wife at 62*, for your counsel on the manuscript. Lastly, I'd like to say a huge thank you to you, Dr Shourabh Mukerji for introducing me to the Ramakrishna Mission. Your generosity from all those years ago was my first step into the type of spiritual inquiry which led to the thoughts in this book.

Introduction

Asemsebe is a Ghanaian word, which roughly translates to "words of wisdom," or "philosophical debate." What follows is a collection of poems, soliloquies, and prose intended to tickle the dormant ears deep within the human psyche. These works are an invitation to ruminate as one's own silent witness. They are conversations with one's self and with the universe at large, in an attempt to make sense of the human condition.

Being That

I am not this.

I am not that.

I am this and that.

I am the canvas and the painting,

though I only show the painting,

for it is in that beauty I marvel.

I am the feeling to be

what you fear not to be.

I am your sense of being,

the very same in him and her;

not another like it, but the very same.

When I say we are one,

it is because of this.

I am that

and you are that.

That is one,

and that is it.

That, is the canvas on which the paints flow,

filling every pore with innumerable color.

Shades as diverse as emotions felt

and experiences gained.

A swirl in one place, a dot in another.

A line here,

crookedness there.

Differing forms, each telling a story,

a chapter, in the one book.

It is through this prism I make visible the rainbows of life.

The paint must appear different,

not the same as the canvas,

otherwise a picture therein, cannot the eye be seen.

It is because of this, that you think yourselves separate.

But the canvas you most definitely are.

That which is so deeply yours,

the sense you have of being,

which feels and says I am.

That is me.

The very same in all,

not another like it,

but the very same *I am*.

When I say we are one, it is because of this.

Forget Me Not

Forgetful are we who live,

frantically frolicking in dense waters of nature manifest.

Pilots, navigating the beast of the mind,

we traverse the twists and turns of the universe

in search of unuttered verses.

Masquerading as separates yet one in the layers;

that is the game of forget me not.

Noble man, child of love,

this divine creature goes on, eons,

oblivious to his majesty.

Infant sparks of the flame of flames which grows in the cycles of celestial clockwork.

Each fills the burgeoning womb of virgin space,

dancing the pirouetting dance of genesis,

until each is none and one is all.

Contented, in the one breath, that vast playground of flames hot and cold, in perfect polarity.

That which moves, tumbling within that in which it is moved, thrilled, by that which wills it to be moved.

For what reason do children play?

Sweet ambrosia!

The same reason does the cycles move.

Endless and unbounded in eternity are the innumerable adventures of the exalted flame.

To sleep, to wake and to play again,

the divine breath palpitates in man with harmonious melody.

Chiming,

Forget me not.

The Silent I

Let this body dissolve from mind.
Let me untangle from delusion,
and be the knower of peace.
These words I say easily,
yet am I to know that reality.
Many a mountain have I climbed,
to make loud that voice within.
Hide not from my cognition,
and draw mockery from a doubting ego.
I grow weary of flesh and bone.
And suspicious of Nature's ways.
Come now and shout;
shout my name that I hear!

With what ears my dear am I?
With what ears can you listen?
I have not a tongue with which to yell,
nor have I hands to bid air fall upon deaf ears.
Yet you look for me in phenomena.
As if I am without your very mind.
Know you not that delusion?
You live, yet death flashes before your eyes.

What gain a farmer who mourns the seeds he sows?

Does he forget they will germinate?

And yet what are you but a seed of God.

And what is God, but the soil in whose embrace you germinate.

What is God but the echoes of the sun and rain,

which nourish your very roots?

Seek me here my dear I am,

for it is your own mind that your eyes reveal.

Wisdom's Gain

A tribute to the healers,
tutors of love who dwell between us.
You have trodden every avenue of life
and tasted of its bittersweet menu.
You have graced every stage, and played every part,
as the drama of life cascades through the ages.

You have been a lover,
and made of the loved a precious flower
through your eye as beholder.
And at cruelty's behest, you have been the unloved,
cast aside, to a cold shoulder.
You have been a thief,
left with no other choice but to shoot the Sheriff.
And you have been that innocence who suffered
at the hand of theft, brought to grief by the thief.

You have felt the chilling cold of lifeless body
as souls have departed amid your embrace.
And you did so with reassuring face;
an eloquent glance of comfort and knowing,
for them that have lost life's great race.

Yours is the cauldron of life itself,

as it must be for all who choose your path.

For who better the healer than the one

who has felt the depth of pain for wisdom's gain.

Who better to counsel on death,

than one who has been at deaths door

and felt the mark of the reapers claw?

Who better than the one who has been to depths of darkness

to ease our darkest hour?

Who better to counsel our shame than the one who has visited

the very pit of shame and carried the parasite of blame upon her back, bled dry, until the deep lights have lit.

Empathy cannot know,

unless it has itself drank from the well it soothes.

This, o' healer, is what you are.

Yours is the bosom of comfort, precisely because your medicine has been the bitterest, and your sorrow, the deepest.

You that have weathered the shadowy tempest of grief

with unwavering belief.

Laid a reef for friend and foe,

and brought hope, as only you know.

The throws of life conspire to make healers of us all.

So that each time we fall, each time we are licked by the flame of deepest pain,

it is a signal that we ourselves are healers in the making.

A necessity for wisdom's gain.

Rock Bottom

Let me sink, to rock bottom.

To the very depths of confusion.

And there may sight be restored,

when delusion finds not a friend.

Let me stand naked, toe to toe with the anguish

which stands guard at rock bottom.

That firm footing, which holds up all above it

when night has fallen upon dreams.

And there I will sit in wonder of unspeakable glory.

Glory, which stands firm beyond the end of tears,

with unwavering shoulders, and feet unmoving.

Let me be muted in amazement of unfathomable something

that eternally is, when nothing is.

Let me lean against your cold face, rock bottom, that the solemn fire which burns within my being may dim no longer,

but begin to give warmth.

Let me be lost in your blinding shadow,

that the latent lamp, which gather dust in my heart,

might flicker again into life,

and the true form of woe be seen for the shadow it surely is.

Rock bottom, shining beacon, which light the path of river and stream into the mighty ocean and ocean to the skies.

Let me ponder your mood, and truth be spoken in asking;

were it not for your temper so brittle,

would I stop to hear your voice?

Come, with your cloak of despair.

Come, and bring with you that anxious temperament,

which is hope in the guise of night.

Come, reveal your unyielding bedrock,

when all have crumbled under the weight of my search.

Law

Send the maker of law to the funeral pyre,
and let rise the lawlessness of peace.

Let each man have justice in his blood,
like the sweet sugar, which flows as one with flower and nectar.

Let none be crushed under the weight of sleepless night.
Let him not lay wake, as bookkeeper of wrong and right,
with the burden of a whip to crack.

Let no deed coerce the hand of another,
to craft in wood the form of gallows.
Then scorn to him apportion for the sins of his brothers.

Let none but each to rule himself,
lest duty be absconded in pursuit of wealth.
And let no one be forced to make of law his bread and butter.

Let trust make kings of the sons of man,
and crown his daughters, queens of all the ages.

Let each be a mirror of truth,
with minds that know not shame nor fear nor guilt.

Let this lawless of laws be spoke and sung
from the tip of each tongue.

Let this lawlessness be spoke and sung,
in your voice for man's release.

Let it fall upon the ears of your heart,
far beyond dead ears, which curse the flesh.

Tide of Power

What armament is carried in power,

that needs must wield, and sufferer does yield?

That universal wine, whose lure has reached all men,

and made of the drunk sober and of the sober, drunk.

What curse is beheld in power, that leaves men eager to devour?

What itch is to be found in power that kills, that thrills,

invokes chills, and has the magnetism to bend will?

What medicine is in power that makes warriors of the meek?

What poison is hidden in power that makes tyrants of the strong, rendering them weak, unable to tame that very asset?

What enormity is in power, that hides, concealed as resistance?

It is no mere absurdity that in having the power to crush,

wielder can resist; a show of reluctance.

For what is in the power to desist, but as much enormity

as the power to persist.

Empires have power built.

Kingdoms have power wilted.

Power has an imprint felt in the devastating heaviness upon

the jilted and the unrequited.

It has forever in the affairs of man dwelt,

spurring on the lover and more still the loved.

Power is the ocean,

whose tide reveals what mere flesh and blood conceal.

The ocean, whose unstoppable wash strips naked

the ego of any it touches.

Power bursts through, bearing witness to hearts truth.

It is the tide of power that recedes to show benevolent pearls,

which lay prevalent under the seabed of life.

But it is also the tide of power

that sneaks away in the dark hour,

leading fishermen astray, who blinded by greed,

pay little attention to its ebb and its flow.

And so, by power's bright light, like a mirror unto all souls,

let each be judged.

Fortune

Wicked and cruel is Fortune,
who makes a noose of dreams
and sends to the gallows
the hopes of tormented souls.
Wicked and cruel is Fortune,
who fills the vista with joyous image,
then makes of quicksand those very shores of happiness.

Thou art wicked o' fortuity,
who favor the virtue of fools,
and cast smiles upon the reprobate,
whose only dreams are malice.
In the wakeful eyes of time
have your deeds been witnessed.
Made true, by those you have chosen,
those very few, who have the many hurt.

You entice me with tenuous offering
of which substance I dare not clutch.
Lest I be fooled again and again
by pomp and gloss of tempting mirage.

Yet wisdom does pray,

that in you I must trust.

You that have long ruled my desperate heart.

You that have longer held dominion over my flailing will.

Only the jester who sits behind reason

shall know why I sit here, begging and pleading,

for your smile upon my wants.

Wicked and cruel are you, O' Fortune,

a trickster and a tease.

In Love's Honor

How I have maimed in love's honor.
The countless flowers I have slain
in the hope of affection.

Forgive my lover's vain nature,
who is fooled by a feast of the eye,
mistaking it for the song of the heart.
Forgive our sweet innocence!
What fools are we, to think there is beauty
in the sacrifice of stem for vanity's course.

And curse my lazy hand, that refuses to work for love.
Curse my brow,
so shy of sweat, that I snap stems and pluck petals
to express what my heart ought to.
Bound by impatience,
I have sought a shortcut to love's desires
and brushed aside the toil of seed for sun and water.

Nature's own art,
cut down in the name of courtship.
Like how I have stolen honey from the diligent bee
to quench my sweet tooth.

Were I to paint a petal,

and put brush to canvas for love.

Were I to attempt a likeness of Mother Nature's work.

Then would I know

the works I have taken for granted,

and so easily slain in love's honor.

Easing Waters

Easing waters of delicate touch,
with hands so soft they yield to the brush,
and yet made strong by the hand of moon,
that patient tool that chisel at rock.
Knead my back of its burdened thought.

Easing waters strong of hold,
in your loss does loose earth scatter.
Bind my sorrow as grains of clay,
mold them into the passing of days,
that I stand strong in the solar kiln.

Easing waters of soothing ways,
take my emotion and carry them away.
Strain them well from these muscles tight,
that I tread light on nature's heirs,
leaving no trace of where I've been.

Easing waters of ocean's tide,
pulling my canoe from side to side.
Still your back, for my journey is long.
Coaxed along by the fervid thread,
that age-old beacon from where I belong.

Easing waters curing of taste,
make haste and quench my thirst,
this clamorous taste that I have of late.
Wash them away like stones to sand,
and in their place make virtue stand.

Easing waters of seasons aplenty,
bring to the desert its unburden,
and fill the cracks of my rainless skin.
Whisper to me that word so sweet,
which sprout leaf and stem from seed;
I too must grow, and to the light seek.

Easing waters thrice of mold,
three degrees of substance fold.
I know your place in cosmic economy,
fecund, as you are nature's own wife.
You alone do fill my veins,
day after day with the stuff of life.

The Wheel of Causes

The maggots and earthworms

spare not the rich or the poor.

Nor indeed our kings and queens,

princes, paupers and yet-to-be's.

To all the muddy waters,

for Mother Nature gives no quarters.

But life there most certainly is,

and to each is their lot.

It is no mistake, nor is it afterthought.

The wheel of cause is spun as it must.

And so, to the one justice,

and the other injustice.

And as there is cause,

so must there be effect.

Yet, by such canny, does wisdom plead;

wield with caution, be yours nurtured by fortune,

lest the cause of providence bear a child of hardship.

Will Power

Upon the battlefield of life and a day,

lay strewn amid mud and clay,

shields and banners of promises broken.

These, the casualties of bargains struck,

between my patient will and me.

And for that, ten thousand wagons ride empty,

stowed there in with the stench of pity.

The passenger that was, now lost,

lured by a cold frost in desires lair.

O' desire, you tuneful siren, I shall make of you a liar yet.

These words have I spoken, time and again,

to loyal audience 'neath the dregs of empty glass.

And poor tomorrow, forever the mule,

laden.

Pall-bearer eternal for my procrastination.

What cruel fate destiny has forced upon unborn shoulders.

And how fortunate today is by comparison.

Born into lavish beds of crimson and purple,

and sung to sleep each night, with the sweetest of lullaby;

tomorrow shall be another day.

If that the petals of my heart

could blossom under silver light,

How useful then, the moon would be,

when she cast shadows in the dead of night

with her borrowed light.

And if the power of my will would blossom,

and be harkened amidst desire's rumble,

she would clip the wings of dragons in victory,

and lay them down at my feet.

But what ears have I to hear?

What courage have I to muster?

Where is the strength in the wind that hurls a ship across the waters, but gives way to the falling leaf?

O' will of wills, grant my wish.

Be for me the worker and the work.

Be the sustenance for my diligence.

Let me bear witness and make strong the path of intuition.

Let the sun reach me where I sleep, and make loose the soil that weighs heavy upon the seeds of my fledgling will.

The Call of Dawn

When the winds of change fall breathless,
shall feather and stone fall alike.
But before that day must necessity rule.
She swings the hand of the zephyr
to fill sails with benevolent winds
or angry gusts, which lengthen our voyage.

And so, does one tree grow tall,
taking root in fertile ground.
And the other short,
finding roots in parched soil.
By the same law does one man err upward,
while the other stumble.
His stride impeded, by restraint opaque,
woven by the hands of forgotten deeds
which rule today by yesterday's sowing.

And there lies the problem.
When pain and anguish swoon the land,
 and men of few toil in mind to fathom why,
while men of far sight burn with a yearning
for a world where symmetry is king.
For that, they berate the cruelty and crookedness of fate.

Whose clandestine hands twist the lay of the land,

causing the many to stumble.

Not until the day when the winds of change shall lay silent,

no more to tug feather and rock with unequal might.

That day when men shall wake one and all,

at the same time to the roosting of dawn.

That day when all rivers and streams shall at once empty into the mighty seas, and the mighty seas to tide in union.

That day when the left-hand steals not from the right,

when mind thinks not for itself,

but for the seven kingdoms of clay.

That high and windless noon shall come,

when ten thousand things return to one.

A Shimmering Veil

A shimmering fabric dances before my eyes.

It is fashioned from the air by the hands of heat.

What once could not be seen,

now appears as a silver sheen.

A gift from temperature.

It is a flowing haze that holds my gaze,

as it traverses the layers of density.

Onwards it goes,

upwards,

in search of pastures higher.

A cunning bait of intrigue these lucent reeds of breeze and swelter.

Like the hunter's flute, it is sent to entice scrutiny;

sent to raise eyes and minds to the heavens.

I take bait, and begin to pry into life

in search of that which casts its shadows.

What else lies beneath the cloak of empty space?

What else lurks beyond these senses five?

What is it that carries the scent of incense even when the air upon which it stood is long gone?

To what intention do heavy clouds hold back, that they not all fall to ground at once, but in droplets as if by colander?

And who am I that can see all this and ask of it questions?
Who am I that bear witness to thoughts in mind as they are born?

But the shimmering haze forever eludes.
Its answers slip through mind,
evading the tip of tongue,
fathomless yet so near.
I reach out to grasp my mercurial temptress,
but fingers slip through her flailing form.
And yet I hop through the land,
chasing haze after haze.
It remains ever in the distance,
a mirage, yet to be known.
The question burns my lip to ask
if ever and ever, can ever be known?

Decisions

The road awaits,

stretched out beyond the eyes.

A picture is painted by the silent artist,

who dwells in the shadow of the mind.

Seduced by far horizons of beyond,

she pegs infinity where she dares.

She dreams,

filling in the unknown, with visions of better.

She prods,

from deep within the silence.

The feet begin to itch.

He knows nothing of the road beyond,

but knows he cannot be where he stands.

Prospect torments the feet, carrying him upon its back,

like the wind to a helpless leaf.

But imagination remedies his cracked soles;

each crack a scar,

the scars of a lifetime, roaming in search of better.

The stomach hesitates. She is born of comfort.

She, the worried mother,

burdened with thoughts of food for her children.

She shackles the feet with an act of love.

But through no fault of hers,

she foils imagination with the anxiety of what if.

And I,

I am the plaintiff.

Perched between passion and the judgment of reason.

I give breath, to passionate dreams of my feet.

And I give credence to the worries of my stomach for good reason.

Caught in two minds, they push and they pull.

Where is the beauty in a wasted life?

The open road asks.

Where is the aegis in a wasted life?

Prudence asks.

And where is the enterprise in a life spent seated on the fence?

Asks the voice of courage.

And in turn I ask of the mind;

Paint me a picture,

which will soothe the worries of my stomach.

And of the stomach, I ask, unshackle my feet.

For I was born to roam the manifest roads of peace.

I was born to soar above clouds,

and nib at nature's fruits when hunger calls.

I was born to suffer not the stale winds of immobility.

I was born to embrace the open pastures that surround the road.

She is my lover.

She is where I want to be.

The Labors of Love

A thundering darkness blows a storm in the seat of my soul.

And the whispers of my heart have fallen silent.

Muzzled by confusion, incipient words miscarry,

and expression is lost in thought,

only to appear as tears and aches and pains and twists of body.

What wind of mind is intent to carry pregnant words astray?

And what ears are there that stand content on hearing,

only to stop shy of response?

These tepid results that have come to bear,

as I bargain with faith, when I plead to the stars at night.

These efforts of mine,

which take root at the wrong solstice.

Spring and harvest pass in silence, leaving behind winters injustice.

Her cold winds blow a cruel fate, intent, on extinguishing the pale tinder that is hope.

Abandoned!

When all I pray is for lightning to fill the darkened sky of mankind.

For the sun to pierce the murky waters of our humanity.

That we may swing in harmony.

That we may celebrate each other in fitting ceremony.

And so, I sit with it,

I breathe with it.

And comfort the hand of hope;

the eternally laden mother in nature's perpetual labor.

I pray that her throes might one day birth.

For I long to be there, to welcome into existence, heirs of incorruptible presence, deserved by the crown of humanity.

A Pearl in The Far Lands

A fog hangs about all things.
A fever for that which treads lightly upon perception.
Yet I abhor not perception.
She has a place in the orders.

But where next?
When the nectar of substance has dried.
Where next?
When the weight of suffering has drowned all joy
like a stone around the necks of the damned.

What then of the urge to become?
That very cause of being,
whose tension brought the spheres into motion.
What then, of this impulse?
When it has become father to greed,
and manifests the coils of injustice?
Must it cling?
And become prisoner to the ticking of time?
And which mortal dare cast judgment upon matters of the dead?
Which sleeping soul would profess to know the burden of the dead?

A thousand times have I journeyed to these far lands.

A thousand times have I sought the pearl,

deep beneath time's sinking sands.

A thousand times have I roamed these tiresome rings of necessity, and crafted pearl after pearl, around these illusions of wakefulness.

The Sleep of Sisyphus

Sleep has come!

Restful sleep has come to you,

O Sisyphus of Corinth.

Lay down your weight!

Bestow upon it a final tumble.

Care not for where last it lands,

for the sun has set upon your days of toil.

Rise with the moon in the west,

and let Ephyra weep.

Let them jeer as well they may!

Care not for the fate of your name upon their lips.

Waste not a bead of sweat on that postulation.

Rest your head where 'er it lay.

Be it warm or cold, from hunger or thirst.

Rest yourself, O king of the mud,

from this world absurd.

Leave her behind, that Persephone,

she who is chained by time.

Look, the many ways she toils for beauty!

Seek not that madness which carve temples in stone

with the movement of water.

Eat not of the fruits from that domain,

lest in that tomb you forever remain.

Fear not the long night, that you should fight a heavy brow.

Let them shut, O Sisyphus of Corinth;

Let them shut, these eyes of mud.

Let them shut,

for they serve not even the blind.

Mortal Coil

Ill waters seep at the roots,

poison, to the fruits of thought!

A great madness hath conjured a manner of fool

who think it prudent, to breed in the midst of slavery.

And yet in the scheme of immortals,

the idle hands of eternity seek knowledge in suffering,

she makes pageantry the ills of life.

To what end, do subtle waters rain heavy upon mortal lands?

And for what do they muddy by design so elaborate?

O what it must be to see this world with timeless eyes,

and make light the throes of life.

To know of things as such,

and pass through death,

as easily as to wake from nightly dreams.

What life then would be lived?

What words then would be spoken in place of bitten tongue?

What heroes would rise in place of a frightened cower?

Alas!

The immortal forever knows,

yet silenced by a mortal coil,

and bound by a mind which thinks itself perishable.

The First and Last Sound

The mighty Sound, a formless river, permeating entirety.

Her presence radiates through all substance subtle and gross.

She seeps through the gaps, even where there is none.

Her essence is a symphony, cloaked with illusive form,

motherly, fatherly, brotherly, and sisterly.

At a glance, she is the animal, the mineral, the plant, the ever-changing stance of permanence.

She is the much more that is presumed gone at the funeral,

but begins again, resumed, as decay embarks on a journey to sustain life.

The last exhalation that evolves into the first.

Ruler, even over the inscrutable domain between breaths.

Hers is the indomitable chord,

the silence within all sound that makes every sound.

She is harmony and discord, the double-edged sword.

In seeing the good, she proclaims I am that.

In seeing sadness and misery, she proclaims I am that.

Seeing the vulture, hovering behind a dying child,

waiting with bated breath, she proclaims I am that.

Seeing the mother who for lack of water, quenches the thirst of her child with saliva, she proclaims I am that.

Seeing the twinkle in the eye of the king, who strangles the water for profit,

she proclaims I am that.

And in seeing the profound beauty disclosed in the smile of a newborn child,

she proclaims I am that.

I am that, I am that, she reverberates.

The melody of what is.

The truth of what is, objective, present and phenomenal.

But she is also the causeless cause, plucking at the strings to produce those effects felt so materially on her own frets.

The note of infinite longevity,

sustained, and audible through all time.

She is grasped so clearly by the many ears of the heart,

but slips through mechanical comprehension,

like fingers through the sands of time.

Her vibration sends the profane descending deep into madness

with faculties, labels, and attempts to tame her for fame and glory.

Her mystical lyric is ever purred, veiled in ancient allegory.

Think it, and she draws near, but speak it, and she becomes it.

O how mighty a sound has built and torn down palaces of grandeur.

Moved earth and stone with a moan and a groan,

a simple tone, sound bites that were once so widely known.

Let us sing!

Sing forward into the past and revive the iconoclast with a sonic blast!

The Sufi dances, in her honor, twirling like the spinning top, displaying how she, the sound enlivens matter.

The dancer being her and the dress being the latter.

See how the dress droops, flat when the spinning is no more.

A symbol of death itself.

The earth spins, gyrating from day into night,

hurtling through space and time,

made alive and humming along with the very same tune.

The Hindu sings as a matter of course, a mantra,

a hymn embodying her sonic force.

The scientist peers under her materialist frock,

eager to discover her curves and her waves.

He takes measurements with atomic clocks

and the finest metronomes,

desperately hoping, to get wind of her baritones.

Many have named her.

They call her the Tao, they call her the way,

they call her the path, they call her oeaohoo,

and much more to this day but she remains just a sound.

A mighty song by itself, playing, hiding itself from itself, fragmenting, into verse and chorus,

composing and re-composing with no particular urgency,

until it can no longer be heard.

Forever gone, and in its place, the peace of God.

A Thousand Little Bells

A thousand little bells ring in my ear.
A thousand little bells, surely from above.
What stops me if not the fear,
to draw nearer to perfect love.
Deceive me not you angels of heaven,
for as I write my ears ring bright.

Curse these eyes who see only doubt.
Come about, amidst my panic lest the sun vanish.

But somehow, methinks I know,
that day and night is sleepless,
like winters in the north.
But I of clay, and stubborn of mind,
doth cling to sorrows bind,
and wrestle with shadows,
as birds do scarecrows.

The Holy Instant

Through the window a magnolia tree stood.

It was the only sight in the dimming light of dusk.

It looked as though covered in cotton wool,

like tiny clouds in nature's womb.

Towering above it stood bare naked trees,

which did not know yet, that it was spring.

And as a heron flew by,

not a word was uttered, but came understanding.

Not a sword swung, but came peace.

And there it was, that which cannot be said.

All my troubles were laid to bed.

I am not a body, nor am I a thing.

I am that I am, a holy thought of Almighty God.

Young Tree

Young tree of the coppice,
would I be a student to thee?
Your very existence is to life a question.
Is yours the one life or many?
I have seen you, breathless, laid bare,
and stood solemn in the dead of winter.
Yet in some other domain, darkened from my eyes,
you continue to live.
Spring sees you wake from that secret slumber,
with untold color and renewed vigor.
Made bold by that secret which hides in your seed.

Young tree of the coppice,
would life be the price to pay, in search of where you go?
That silent place, where you dwell,
shrouded, through the ages by your innermost of rings.
I look upon your works with second sight,
and see eternity in evergreen canopy.
Bourne aloft are your leaves, that know so well the seven suns,
they need no medium to digest his golden rays.
Your unseen roots move like serpents,
knowing the hidden depth of Mother Earth.
They meander, shrouded in cold and darkness,

unafraid, to drink of Her secret milk;

turning her minerals to fruitful gold.

Young tree of the coppice,

masters of time are you,

gentle of spirit who move as steadily as the heavenly stars.

You have lived long enough, to see Orion lift his mighty bow, releasing his arrow across the night sky

to strike that great target, beyond my eyes.

You do all your living, unbeknownst to man,

who'd think himself your lord and master.

And yet you remain still, steadfast with love,

as you give to him the breath of life.

And bear for him countless fruit

which fill his very being with stuff of life.

Teach me, o' young tree you voice of God,

for today, I shall be your humble student.

Innocence

The spirit of a mother bird soared above the land. She was free from the shackles of substance. And having gained sight, she could see into the hearts of those still adorned with mortal garments.

She felt not pain or sorrow, though she had known them.

Her heart remained still, even as she swooped down into the valley where her child lay, separated from earthly mother, awaiting a fate of the dreamless sleep. She sat atop a cocoa tree, that she might bring comfort to her fading chick.

It was here that she saw an orphan boy, far in the distance, skipping through the trees. His footsteps alight with innocence. His was a bright smile, like the diamond specs of light, which garnish the sea at night. The mother bird saw into his heart, and there dwelt purity, immaculate and untouched by the wrenching hands of longing and intemperance. His mind was as the first of the morning's dew which grace the blades of Mother Nature's grass; yet to be ruffled by the footsteps of drama. His conscience was pristine. Untouched by the nibs of life and not yet engraved upon by the trials of time.

The boy drew near to the shadow of the cocoa tree, under which lay the dying babe. She was weak, pink and sporadic with feathers. Her eyelids clenching shut, with the heaviness of not long for this world. On seeing this, the boy's heart quickened. He became filled with sorrow as the thorn of sadness prickled. Having no answer, innocence cowered. He raised the babe into his sun-soaked palms. In there, her slowing heart found comfort as the boy began a somber walk, eyes fixed upon the departing bird.

Far in the distance came another boy, fit, running and spurred on by a wailing crowd. In his soul dwelt also purity, immaculate and uninjured by desire. But virtue came to hear the sweet whispers of appetite; beaten upon it by the tongues of the gathered folk.

The boy's feet moved fast. His body brushed aside the impeding air to gain advantage against it. His teeth grimaced and his arms flailed with raw determination.

Hearing the noise, the orphan boy was jolted from his sorrowful trance. Just at that moment, he awoke into the eyes of his sweat clad compatriot, whose determined hands reached down to snatch a pot of jewels from his feet. A bounty of jewels placed there by the impartiality of providence.

The ecstatic boy, now panting within the embrace of luck, disappeared off into the crowd laughing with a jubilant stupor. The gathered people celebrated his windfall and praised his gumption.

The orphan boy's heart boiled, as purity became stained with anger and injustice. And the hand of anger, at revenge's bidding, killed the babe with a sharp clench.

Soon after, innocence shrieked as it bowed into great remorse. Three spirits now rose above the cocoa trees, soaring far into the clouds. And with them, the understanding of the shadow of man, and the reason for his lengthy passage through the ages.

Age of The Reluctant Heart

To take the weight off her feet, a nomad woman sat alone in the desert. Her hands rested in her bosom clutching a bundle of seeds.

They had been a last gift to her from her departed husband.

She sat quietly, her face veiled by a scarf as she contemplated where to sow them. She considered whether she had the strength to endure the lashes of the desert which was set to torment, in her search of fecundity.

Amid thought, she watched in the distance, her children at play,

gallivanting in and out of the drapes of their caravan.

She watched them through the heat, which rippled the atmosphere

into a glossy expanse, ever animated, yet depicting solidity of forms behind it. Through this etheric echo, she no longer saw children but saw gods at play.

They cast lots.

Throwing sticks of fate onto the heaving fabric of the atmospheric miasma. Each lot was a life to be lived, lives, of all forms and measure. Some were bejeweled with riches, gleaning and sparkling with provident blessings. Others were rotten, filled with decay, which dwindled into misery and sleepless nights on hardened floors.

Some were truly so, while others were only so in but appearance.

The excited children rushed to grab lots.

Some of them, older, paused and gave thought weighing one against the other. The younger ones, propelled by exuberance hurled themselves through the gates of fate, head first as they trod backward armed with the brittle discernment of youth.

One child, the youngest, held back.

She was reluctant to draw her lot, to take her pick of myriad lives.

Unbeknownst to her, curiosity watched through her mother's eyes

as she watched her siblings play and took note of their countless ways.

The one, whose life was filled with riches, hauled it all into his breast. Careful to drop none, lest his future should lack for want.

He hailed himself as lord of the lands since he was the richest, and he spat at the one with nothing, labeling him lazy, and a thing to detest.

The one whose lot had nothing filled his heart with anger and hatred. He lamented the works of the rich and masked his whole life with scornful thoughts of loathing and revenge.

The one with castles barred his gates to the rough sleeper, even when he had rooms filled only with the silence of the air.

He dined alone each evening, feasting with his eyes, which by far dwarfed his stomach.

The one with the congregation, ordered his gatherers to give what little they had, that they may be saved from a fate eternally bleak in a land far beyond. He preached sharing and brotherhood, but held on tightly to what he had acquired from his brothers.

The one, who was lawmaker, twisted those very laws to aid his friends, and employed it against his enemies for gains.

He saw no wickedness in his deeds, and thought himself higher than his own law.

The one whose lot it was to protect turned his weapon to, and drew blood from those he was tasked to protect. He attacked them at the bidding of handsome reward.

The one with medicine kept his secrets to himself as plagues reigned supreme all around him. Affording a cure to only those who would cross his palms with silver and gold.

The one who was set to teach filled the heads of eager children with ideas that corrupted them and caused them to pillage their neighbors for glory.

The one who was a father laid hand upon the mother of his children and fed his anger with drink. The mother killed her own, that they might not flourish in bondage.

The son sought to be like his father, abandoned responsibility and apportioned the blame onto his father for what he had become.

The daughter escaped the mother's snare, but lacking wisdom, mistook a want for possession for happiness, and married not for love but for riches.

The one with justice in his heart, battered by injustice sought solace from all and did nothing, living his days alone in a mountainous tomb.

And the one who was elected to lead, permitted it all to happen, caring only for himself and for what portion of others property was due him. Concealed as taxes, he collected from all under pain of death and counted his riches.

The youngest child wept as she saw her siblings play. One by one they returned from the playground, wearied, stained with the dirt of play but carried with them no remorse.

Reluctance grew weak in her heart as it was vanquished by the will of truth. When they next drew lots, she jumped in and snatched the lot of Queen, so that power did not fall into the hands of malice.

She would be Queen of wisdom and rule only with love because of what she had seen.

When the mother had witnessed this, she knew that her husband had not died in vain. She rose from her rest and made haste for the only oasis in the desert. Enduring the lashes of the desert, she would plant and nurture the seeds, because she had seen the face of hope.

www.ingramcontent.com/pod-product-compliance
Lightning Source LLC
Chambersburg PA
CBHW061513040426
42450CB00008B/1592